AUSTRALIA

It is difficult to grasp the vastness of the Australian continent and the distance between centres such as Sydney and Perth, Melbourne and Brisbane, Adelaide and Darwin. Modern means of transport cut travelling time to a minimum, but, enclosed in their airconditioned cocoons, travellers of today may not have leisure or opportunity to see and enjoy the scenery while journeying. To discover the Great Barrier Reef, or Uluru, or Sydney Harbour, or Kakadu, or the Flinders Ranges, or Tasmania's south-western wilderness, or Western Australia's wildflowers, is to accumulate memories to last a lifetime. However, en route to any of these places that the traveller passes through, or flies over, are many other places of great interest and unique fascination.

So a trip from Sydney to Melbourne will give the opportunity to see the south coast of New South Wales, or to explore Canberra and then travel the Murray River on a paddlewheeler. A visit to the Great Barrier Reef can include exploration of the rainforested mountains of the hinterland, with their scenic waterfalls and thriving small towns. On the way from Darwin to Adelaide, trips off the highway can take in the rugged splendour of Katherine Gorge and the MacDonnell Ranges, the awe-inspiring giant rocks of Uluru and Kata Tjuta, and the stark beauty of the Flinders Ranges.

In Australia, a journey should be enjoyed for its own sake, and to travel observantly is often as satisfying as to arrive. Some destinations are recorded in this book, as are some of the wonderful scenes to be enjoyed along the way.

Above: *The Sydney Opera House and a Manly ferry seen as the golden glow of sunrise lights Sydney Harbour.*
Below: *Sydney Harbour Bridge at dawn, viewed across Campbells Cove.*

Top: *Brave souls enjoy the view over the Opera House, the Harbour and the city from the top of Sydney Harbour Bridge.*
Above, left to right: *Faunal and floral emblems of New South Wales: Laughing Kookaburra, Platypus and Waratah.*

NEW SOUTH WALES

SYDNEY

The colony of New South Wales was founded on 26 January 1788, when the officers, marines and convicts of the First Fleet arrived on the shores of Sydney Harbour, a place long inhabited by the indigenous Eora people. Free settlers soon followed and settlement spread across the Great Dividing Range to the west, and along the coastal plains to north and south. Today, over four million people live in Sydney, capital of the State of New South Wales. Multicultural, sophisticated and a centre of commerce and culture, Sydney extends around a magnificent harbour, where international shipping takes its turn with pleasure and commuter craft, and, occasionally, holidaying whales. The soaring Harbour Bridge and the graceful shells of the Opera House are landmarks that symbolise this first of Australia's capitals, grown to reign proudly as one of the world's great cities.

Sydney's first suburbs grew up around Sydney Cove and the sandstone outcrops of the area known as The Rocks, where restoration has today recreated the atmosphere of Old Sydney Town. The colonial buildings contrast with the shining towers of the city's business centre. West of the Bridge, Darling Harbour offers exhibition, convention and shopping complexes, as well as Sydney Aquarium, the National Maritime Museum and other fascinating venues. East of the Bridge are the Opera House and the beautiful Royal Botanic Gardens, thriving on the site where early settlers first attempted to grow crops. The Harbour itself is Sydney's playground: outside its sheltered waters around thirty ocean beaches offer great surf, seaside walks and plenty of places to eat and play.

Top: *The Tasman Sea foams against the sandstone cliffs of Diamond Bay, Vaucluse, with Sydney Harbour and city behind.*
Above, left: *A view over Rose Bay, Double Bay and Rushcutters Bay to the city.* **Above, right:** *In the Royal Botanic Gardens.*

eft: *The sweep of Manly Beach.*   **Top, right:** *A retired Manly ferry and the Bounty replica moored at Darling Harbour.*
, left: *The Bounty replica proceeds towards Fort Denison and the Opera House.*   **Above, right:** *Bondi Beach and Sydney's eastern suburbs.*
: *Sydney city skyline, seen beyond the Harbour, Royal Botanic Gardens and the grounds of Government House.*

Top: *The sandstone ramparts of the Blue Mountains form a natural barrier between the coastal plains and the fertile inland plains.*
Above, left: *One of the Blue Mountains' famous gardens, at Cherry Cottage, Mount Wilson.* **Above, right:** *The upper cascade of Wentworth Falls.*
Below, left to right: *Katoomba – Scenic Railway plunges into the valley; Scenic Skyway soars past the Three Sisters; Sceniscender gives a fine view of the Jamison Valley.*

Above: *The Three Sisters overlook the spectacular Jamison Valley, near Katoomba. Legend says that, in order to save them from a Bunyip, three girls were turned into stone by their father, who then lost the means of returning them to their original forms.*

THE BLUE MOUNTAINS

Just west of Sydney are the rugged gorges, sandstone cliffs and wild vistas of the Blue Mountains, so-called because of the colour haze created by light rays passing through mists of eucalypt oil rising from the forests of gum trees. Sydneysiders have relaxed in the temperate climate and enjoyed the wild places of these mountains for many years. Today, many other visitors also experience the diverse wildlife, spectacular scenery and beautiful gardens of the region. A number of national parks offer multiple attractions for bushwalkers, birdwatchers, photographers and nature lovers, while lookouts, walkways and people-movers such as the Sceniscender, Scenic Railway and Scenic Skyway offer exhilarating ways for everyone to discover the grandeur of the mountains.

North of Sydney   **Above:** *The vineyards of the Hunter Valley produce some of the world's finest wines.*
Below, clockwise from top left: *Pleasure and fishing craft in safe moorings at Coffs Harbour; Crystal Shower Falls, Dorrigo National Park; Nobbys Beach and lighthouse, Newcastle; Mount Warning, a remaining fragment of the Big Scrub, in its own national park just south of the Queensland–New South Wales border.*

The fertile coast of New South Wales lies between the scenic eastern slopes of the Great Dividing Range, replete with spectacular wild rivers, gorges and forests, and the Pacific Ocean.

North from Sydney, rivers such as the Hunter make their way to the sea through verdant valleys, whose abundant vineyards produce premier wines. The seaside resorts of the Central Coast and the Northern Rivers district are year-round attractions and centres for rich agricultural districts.

To Sydney's south are forests protected in national parks, and green and pleasant pastures, where contented dairy cattle produce creamy milk that is transformed into gourmet cheeses and other delicacies. Wollongong, a port, university city and industrial centre, looks southward to a chain of seaside towns whose fishing fleets are at sea daily when the weather permits.

South of Sydney **Clockwise, from top left:** *Flagstaff Point, lighthouses and harbour, Wollongong; Fitzroy Falls on the Illawarra Escarpment in Morton National Park; Merimbula is surrounded by Merimbula, Top and Back Lakes; Narooma, on Wagonga Inlet.*

Above: *Parliament House, on Capital Hill, Canberra. Much of the complex is below ground. Lake Burley Griffin and Black Mountain, crowned by the Telstra Tower, are seen in the distance.*

AUSTRALIAN CAPITAL TERRITORY

CANBERRA

Unlike most of the world's national capitals, Canberra was constructed to a plan rather than just allowed to grow. It was founded in 1913 after much argument between the States as to its site, and was designed by architect Walter Burley Griffin as a city in which it was possible to achieve "directness and speed in communication between all points". The Molonglo River basin eventually became Lake Burley Griffin, which is surrounded by many of Australia's most impressive public buildings, and is overlooked by the Parliament House, opened in 1988. Canberra's name derives from an Aboriginal term meaning "meeting place", and, while the city, being the seat of the Australian Federal Parliament, brings the country's elected representatives together, it also attracts visitors to the national art gallery, museum and other institutions, and to its magnificent gardens and lake.

Clockwise, from top left: *An aerial view of City Hill and Commonwealth Avenue Bridge over Lake Burley Griffin; the Royal Bluebell, floral emblem of the ACT; the Gang-gang Cockatoo is the Territory's faunal emblem; entrance to the Australian Institute of Sport; Old Parliament House.*
Below: *Tulips and pansies blooming in Commonwealth Park during Floriade, Canberra's spring festival.*

Above: *The Australian War Memorial, which is approached along Anzac Parade, stands at the foot of Mount Ainslie.*

Below, left: *The National Museum of Australia is on Acton Peninsula on the shores of Lake Burley Griffin.*

Below, right: *A courtyard inside the museum.*

EXCITING CANBERRA

Lake Burley Griffin's landscaped surrounds form a wonderful recreational area. Buildings such as the National Library and the National Museum ornament its foreshore, while the Captain Cook Memorial Water Jet and the Carillon are landmarks. On the lake's city shore, Commonwealth Park leads Canberra's springtime explosion of colour when tulips and other flowers burst into blossom in time for Floriade. The Australian National Botanic Gardens, on the slopes of Black Mountain, contain a marvellous display of flora, while Tidbinbilla, a 40-minute drive from the city, is home to many native animals as well as the Deep Space Communication Complex.

Top, left: *The Carillon stands on Aspen Island, Lake Burley Griffin.*   **Top, right:** *Captain Cook Water Jet and National Library.*
Above, left: *In the National Botanical Gardens.*   **Above, right:** *Tidbinbilla's Canberra Deep Space Communication Complex.*

Top, left to right: *Queensland's faunal and floral emblems, the Koala, the Cooktown Orchid and the Brolga.*
Above: *The view of Brisbane city across the Brisbane River where it winds around Kangaroo Point.*

QUEENSLAND

BRISBANE

The State of Queensland covers one-fifth of the mainland and encompasses nearly every type of Australian landscape. Brisbane, the capital, is in the south-east. To the south is the fabulous Gold Coast, northwards lies the burgeoning Sunshine Coast. The Brisbane River curls through the heart of Brisbane city, passing under a succession of bridges on its way to Moreton Bay and the Pacific Ocean. Bordered with green spaces and promenades, and highlighting South Bank Parklands across from the city centre, the river is a focus for Brisbane's outdoor lifestyle. Footpath cafés and courtyard restaurants, parks and gardens, markets and open-air cultural events all take full advantage of the city's subtropical climate, with its warm, moist summers and sunny, temperate winters.

Top: *The lagoon at South Bank Parklands, a popular relaxation area across the river from Brisbane's city centre.*
Above, left: *The Goodwill footbridge joins South Bank to Gardens Point in the city.*   **Above, right:** *The Story Bridge connects Kangaroo Point to the city and Fortitude Valley.*
Below, left: *The lookout above the lake in the Roma Street Parkland.*   **Below, right:** *The main entrance of Brisbane City Hall, which opens onto King George Square.*

Above, left: *Sunrise seen across a Gold Coast beach.* **Above, right:** *Chalahn Falls, in the rainforests of Lamington National Park, south-east Queensland.*
Below: *A view northward along the Gold Coast from Broadbeach. To the left of the picture, the Nerang River winds behind the beachside buildings.*

Just south of Brisbane, along a multi-lane motorway, lies the Gold Coast, Australia's most popular tourist destination. Its golden beaches stretch for 40 kilometres and the Coast lifestyle can be simple or sophisticated, depending on the holiday-maker's taste. The attractions include sun, sand and surf, sailing and fishing, all sorts of athletic activities, theme parks, and, just a short drive away, the green rainforests and shining waterfalls of the Lamington Plateau.

Queensland's Sunshine Coast stretches to the north of Brisbane, along a line of magnificent beaches extending from Caloundra to Double Island Point. Bribie Island lies offshore, and inland are the spectacular peaks of the Glass House Mountains and the cool slopes of the Blackall Range. Places along this seacoast have names that echo the sounds of sea breezes and ocean – Cooloola, Mooloolaba, Noosa, Maroochydore – and they are noted for their hospitality.

Clockwise, from top left: *Maroochydore, on the estuary of the Maroochy River; Laguna Bay and the Noosa River estuary, Noosa; Kings Beach, Caloundra; the Wharf, Mooloolaba.* **Below:** *The Glass House Mountains seen from Bribie Island.*

Clockwise, from top left: *Fraser Island, the world's largest sand island; Humpback Whales on their migration up the coast to mate and give birth; a Fraser Island Dingo; Shute Harbour, gateway to the Whitsunday Islands.*

TRAVELLING NORTH

Just north of the Sunshine Coast lies World-Heritage-listed Fraser Island. Enormous sand dunes, freshwater lakes, rainforest creeks, breathtaking beaches and legendary fishing spots make this a holiday-makers' paradise. The wildlife includes Dingos, which can be observed but should not be encouraged by feeding. The eastern migration route of Humpback Whales, the numbers of which are growing every year, runs up the coast past Fraser. North of the Tropic of Capricorn, which is straddled by the city of Rockhampton, lie Mackay and the Whitsunday Islands. Heading north, the city of Townsville is the unofficial capital of Tropical North Queensland, and Hinchinbrook Island, off Cardwell, is a 390 square kilometre national park of scenic grandeur. Further north still, the tropical city of Cairns provides a base to explore the Atherton Tableland, the awesome rainforests of the hinterland and the wonders of the Great Barrier Reef. Visitors who push on up the peninsula come to the resort town of Port Douglas, the Wet Tropics World Heritage Area and, finally, Cape York.

Top, left: *Strolling the tide line on Hinchinbrook Island.*   **Above, left:** *Pleasure and fishing craft moored safely at Port Douglas.*
Above, right: *Hill Inlet, Whitsunday Island, in the Whitsunday Group.*   **Below:** *The Strand, Townsville's oceanfront promenade.*

Above, left: *A train passes Stoney Creek Falls on the historic Kuranda Scenic Railway.*
Top, right: *The Red-eyed Tree-frog lives in the forest canopy.* **Above, right:** *A male Cairns Birdwing Butterfly.*
Below, left: *Cape Tribulation in Daintree National Park, part of the Wet Tropics of Queensland World Heritage Area.*
Below, right: *The Eclectus Parrot (this is a female) lives in tropical rainforest.* **Bottom, right:** *Rainforest and beach, Dunk Island.*

Queensland's north-eastern rainforests are relics of primeval times when Australia was far wetter than it is today. They are treasure-houses of exotic plants and remarkable animals, their buttress-trunked trees, palms, vines, streams and waterfalls forming unique ecosystems. In places, such as at Cape Tribulation, the rainforest surges right down to the sea, separated from coral reefs by only a slender strip of silver sand. The Great Barrier Reef, a marvel of nature, stretches south for 2000 kilometres from Torres Strait. It consists of about 2500 individual reefs, 250 continental islands and some 70 coral cays. The reef's admirers may stay at an island resort, sail the Coral Sea, or take part in one of the many day trips or cruises on offer in ports from Cairns and Port Douglas south to Bundaberg.

Clockwise, from top left: *Orange-fin Anemonefish and its host anemone; savouring the fascination of the Great Barrier Reef; popular Green Island, off Cairns; craft moored in Trinity Bay, Cairns; Green Turtles are common in reef waters.*

Above: *The Museum of Victoria opposite the Royal Exhibition Building in Carlton Gardens. The Melbourne Cricket Ground (MCG) is shown in the distance at left.*

VICTORIA

MELBOURNE

Occupying less than three per cent of the area of Australia, the State of Victoria includes a wide variety of landscapes and lifestyles. Places of pristine beauty, areas of natural excitement, surf and snow, beaches, mountains, even deserts – Victoria has all these attractions. Melbourne, the State capital, has been described as the world's best-preserved nineteenth-century city, but it is also a great centre of commerce and industry that offers the latest in entertainment and international trends. While it retains a very Australian identity, it has benefited from the cultural contributions of many nations. Within easy reach are the Dandenong Ranges, the Mornington and Bellarine Peninsulas and historic gold-rush towns such as Ballarat and Bendigo. Further afield are the Great Ocean Road, the rugged Grampians, the paddlewheelers of the Murray River, the great granite peninsula known as Wilsons Promontory, and the forests and snowfields of the Australian Alps.

Top left: *Victoria's floral emblem, the Common Heath.* **Above left:** *The State's faunal emblem, Leadbeater's Possum.* **Above right:** *Flinders Street Station and one of Melbourne's famous trams.* **Below, left:** *Melbourne seen across Port Phillip Bay from St Kilda Pier.* **Below, right:** *A view down the Yarra River towards Princes Bridge.*

Top, left: *A view across St Patrick's Cathedral to Parliament House.* **Top, right:** *Crown Entertainment Complex and Casino ready to welcome patrons.*

Above, left: *Lygon Street, Carlton, is a bustling centre of restaurants and cafés.* **Above, right:** *Looking across the Shrine of Remembrance to Melbourne city.*

Below: *Melbourne's trams, retained for their historical interest when the rest of the world was digging up tram-tracks, provide fast, easy, clean and green transport around the cit*

The Yarra River winds serenely through the vineyards and farms of the Yarra Valley to Melbourne's suburbs, the city itself and Port Phillip Bay. With a population of about three million, Melbourne is noted for its magnificent parks and gardens, the excellence of its public transport, and the friendly, sports-loving nature of its inhabitants. It is also culturally vibrant, with plenty of theatres, a lively music scene and wonderful artistic venues such as the Arts Centre, the National Gallery of Victoria and the impressive Museum of Victoria. On the city's southern edge lies Port Phillip Bay and its peninsulas. At the mouth of Westernport Bay is Phillip Island, famed for its Little Penguins and Australian Fur-seals, while to the south-east, jutting into Bass Strait, lie the great wild areas of Wilsons Promontory, affectionately known to generations of nature lovers and bushwalkers as "The Prom".

Top: *South East Point, Wilsons Promontory National Park.* **Above, left:** *Little Penguins can be seen on beaches on Phillip Island and other parts of the coastline.* **Above, right:** *An Australian Fur-seal swims gracefully through a bed of kelp.*

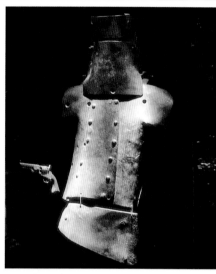

Clockwise, from top left: *Sovereign Hill, Ballarat, re-creates a town of the gold-rush era; Emmylou, a paddlesteamer based on the Murray River at Echuca; Ned Kelly's armour is displayed in Melbourne's Old Gaol; Puffing Billy steaming between Belgrave and Emerald Lake, in the Dandenong Ranges.*
Below: *The Twelve Apostles stand in the sea-haze off the limestone cliffs of Port Campbell National Park, west of Melbourne.*

Top: *The Balconies overlook Victoria Valley and the Serra Range in the Grampians, western Victoria.*
Above: *Lakes Entrance cuts through Ninety Mile Beach, a sandbar buffer between the Gippsland Lakes and the ocean.*

HERITAGE, HISTORIC AND NATURAL

The second half of the nineteenth century was a turbulent time in the colony of Victoria. Gold-rushes brought prosperity and spawned bushrangers such as the Kelly gang. Wealth from timber and wool founded a fleet of paddlewheelers on the River Murray and encouraged the spread of railways. Victoria in the twenty-first century celebrates its rich, but sometimes violent history.

It is equally rich in natural beauty, including the stacks of limestone that defy the stormy waves of the Southern Ocean in Port Campbell National Park. Further west, the Great Dividing Range ends in the spectacular peaks and gorges of the Grampians. On the other, eastern, side of the State are the diverse pleasures of the Gippsland coastal lowlands. A popular tourist trail winds through the area, which includes Australia's largest system of internal waterways, stunning beaches, lush farmlands, and historic towns and homesteads.

TASMANIA

HOBART

The island of Tasmania is surrounded by seas rich in marine life, blessed with fertile soils and temperate climate, and containing some of the world's last remaining untouched wilderness. In the south-east, the State capital, Hobart, standing on a superb harbour on the Derwent River estuary, is Australia's second-oldest city. For years after it was founded in 1803 it was a roaring port for sealers and whalers, then a prosperous outlet for agricultural produce. The days when convicts were sent to Van Diemen's Land left an indelible mark on Tasmania.

The island also has a "northern capital", the city of Launceston, on the River Tamar. Across the north from east to west are delightful towns and wonderful scenery; the wildness of the west makes it less accessible, but its beauty is breathtaking.

Clockwise, from top left: *Hobart and the mouth of the Derwent River viewed from the top of Mount Wellington; fishing boats moored in Constitution and Victoria Docks, Sullivans Cove, Hobart; Tasmanian Blue Gum, the State's floral emblem; Tasmanian Devils are unique to Tasmania.*

Above, left: *Richmond Bridge, built by convicts between 1823 and 1825, overlooked by St John's Church.* **Above, right:** *Cattle grazing in pasture above Stanley, with The Nut in the background.* **Below, left:** *Sailing dinghies on Cataract Gorge, Launceston.* **Below, right:** *Lyons Cottage, Stanley, where former Prime Minister of Australia J.A. Lyons was born.* **Bottom, right:** *The waterfront, Strahan.*

Above, left: *A cirque lake in the Arthur Range, Southwest National Park.* **Top, right:** *The Hazards seen over Coles Bay on the Freycinet Peninsula.*
Above, right: *Lake Rodway, Cradle Mountain–Lake St Clair National Park.* **Below:** *Liffey Falls, Liffey Falls State Reserve, south-west of Launceston.*

Many of Tasmania's wild places, some listed as World Heritage areas, have remained virtually unchanged for millions of years and contain plants common when dinosaurs roamed the earth. Others bear the scars of past ice ages, when glaciers tore away the topsoil and gouged out hollows that today form lakes. Some regions have been transformed by logging, or by clearing for farmland or pasture, and the fertile soils of the north and north-west have been sown to many crops, including medicinal poppies and sweet-smelling lavender. The Tasman Peninsula, 100 kilometres from Hobart, is the site of the island's most poignant ruins. Past narrow Eaglehawk Neck is Port Arthur, once the cruellest of penitentiaries. From 1830 to 1877 it was a dreaded place of punishment where many convicts suffered and some died, to be buried in unmarked graves on the Isle of the Dead.

Top: *The ruins of the chapel at Port Arthur Penitentiary, once a dreaded place of punishment for re-offending convicts.*
Above: *Lavender is one of the specialty crops grown in Tasmania's fertile soils and temperate climate.*

SOUTH AUSTRALIA

ADELAIDE

A State with no use of convict labour to colour its history, South Australia has enormous arid areas and one well-watered and fertile corner, the south-east. Here stands the State capital, Adelaide, an elegant city centred around five squares and a multitude of green spaces. The River Torrens widens to Torrens Lake as it passes through the city, and it is a short distance to Gulf St Vincent lined with beaches, of which Glenelg can be reached by Adelaide's one remaining tram. Adelaide hosts an internationally famous biennial Festival of Arts and other cultural events. The city's "boulevard of learning", North Terrace, is home of the Adelaide University, the South Australian Museum, Art Gallery, State Library, Festival Centre, Botanic Gardens and casino.

Top: *An aerial view of Adelaide, with the River Torrens at centre.* **Above, left and right:** *The floral and faunal emblems of South Australia: Sturt's Desert Pea and the Southern Hairy-nosed Wombat.*

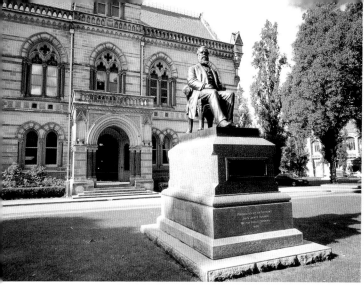

Top, left: *The Mitchell Building, Adelaide University, North Terrace.*   **Top, right:** *The view from inside the main gates of the Botanic Gardens of Adelaide to the Botanic Hotel.*
Above: *Adelaide's Festival Centre, a multipurpose complex for the arts, seen across Torrens Lake.*
Below, left: *Adelaide's seaside suburb, Glenelg, and the Glenelg Jetty.*   **Below, right:** *The Summit, Mount Lofty, and Cleland Conservation Park, near Adelaide.*

Top, left: *Vineyards at McLaren Vale, in one of South Australia's premier wine-producing regions.*   **Top, right:** *A view of vines and pastures in the Barossa Valley.*
Above, left: *Remarkable Rocks, Flinders Chase National Park, Kangaroo Island.*   **Above, right:** *An Australian Sea-lion at Seal Bay Conservation Park, Kangaroo Island.*
Below: *The historic Hahndorf Inn, Main Street, Hahndorf, a charming town in the Adelaide Hills.*

From Coonawarra, south of Adelaide, to the Clare Valley, north of the city, the Mediterranean climate and the soils of south-eastern South Australia are ideal for growing grapes and making wines. Many vineyards and other farms in the Barossa Valley and Adelaide Hills were founded by Germans taking refuge from religious persecution in Europe: towns such as Hahndorf retain much of their original character and the area is noted for its festive celebrations of good food and wines. North again are farmlands and the breathtaking vistas of the Flinders Ranges. Where there is water, crops and animals are raised for food: fine produce comes from the lands that benefit from the flows of the mighty River Murray before it empties into Encounter Bay. Reached by ferry or by air, Kangaroo Island is a place to enjoy both the scenery and the wildlife that flourishes in sanctuary from feral predators.

Top: *An aerial view of Wilpena Pound, a vast, shallow basin in Flinders Ranges National Park.*
Above, left: *Emus are common in South Australia's Outback.* **Above, right:** *Approaching the Flinders Ranges.*

Top: *People of Darwin enjoy the gentle sea waters while the sun sinks and the heat leaches from the air.*
Above: *Pandanus and casuarina trees silhouetted against Fannie Bay, Darwin, at sunset.*

THE NORTHERN TERRITORY

DARWIN

Some places in the Northern Territory, such as Uluṟu, the mighty red monolith, and the wetlands and waterfalls of Kakadu National Park, have become icons for Australia. Others are hardly known to anyone but the indigenous people who have been their guardians for untold ages. It is still a land of legends, where nature can overpower the most cunning efforts of humankind, as Cyclone Tracy proved in 1974 when it devastated the Territory's capital city, Darwin. Darwin has been rebuilt since then and presents a model image of a modern city, but it is still a place to appreciate the power and beauty of nature. Where else would crowds gather on the beach each evening in the dry season to applaud the sun setting in scarlet and crimson glory over a darkening sea?

Above, left: *Florence Falls, in Litchfield National Park, within easy driving distance of Darwin.*
Top, right: *Limestone formations, Tawallah Range, Gulf of Carpentaria.* **Above, right:** *The sandstone Arnhem Land escarpment is the northern edge of a great plateau.*
Below, left to right: *The Northern Territory's avian emblem is the Wedge-tailed Eagle; Sturt's Desert Rose is its floral emblem; the popular Frilled Lizard.*

In Kakadu National Park **Top, left:** *Nourlangie Rock seen over Anbangbang Billabong.* **Top, right:** *Aboriginal rock art in Anbangbang Gallery, Nourlangie Rock.*
Above, left: *Birdwatching on the wetland at Yellow Water.* **Above, right:** *The Saltwater Crocodile is the major predator in coastal rivers and extensive wetlands.*
Below, left: *Twin Falls in the wet season, where Jim Jim Creek tumbles over the escarpment.* **Below, right:** *Looking to the East Alligator River floodplains from Ubirr Lookout.*

Kakadu National Park lies 250 kilometres from Darwin along the Arnhem Highway. It is managed by its traditional owners, the Gagudju people, in collaboration with the Commonwealth organisation, Environment Australia. This is a world of dramatic sandstone cliffs, over which, in the wet season, waterfalls thunder to fill the coastal wetlands below. It is a land of rainforested gorges, stone outliers, lotus lilies and Saltwater Crocodiles. Indigenous people have lived here for tens of thousands of years, and their art testifies to the strength of their culture and their long association with the land.

The Stuart Highway runs south from Darwin, passing by Nitmiluk National Park, where 13 red-walled gorges have been carved from sandstone by the Katherine River. To the east of the highway are the cattle properties of the Barkly Tableland; west is the Victoria River Region. A thousand kilometres south of Darwin, the giant boulders known as the Devils Marbles salute travellers.

Top: *The Katherine River flows through Katherine Gorge in Nitmiluk National Park.*
Above: *The Devils Marbles, huge granite boulders, lie in a conservation reserve beside the Stuart Highway.*

Above: *Uluru (Ayers Rock) stands alone in the red sands. In the foreground, a stand of Honey Grevillea bears witness to the passing, some weeks before the picture was taken, of a rare heavy rainstorm.*

THE RED CENTRE

The burnished colours of Central Australia owe their being to the thin layer of iron oxide that coats each tiny grain of sand and glows in the rays of the sun. In the centre of the continent, the MacDonnell Ranges stretch for 400 kilometres in parallel ridges, slashed across by gorges carved from the sandstone by long-vanished rivers. The waterholes that remain in these ravines attract wildlife, and visitors, to the MacDonnells. In the south-west corner of the Northern Territory is Uluru–Kata Tjuta National Park. Classified as a World Heritage Site, it centres on two stone monuments. Uluru (Ayers Rock) stands 348 metres above the desert and is 3.6 kilometres long and 2.4 kilometres wide. Two-thirds of this mighty rock lie beneath the sand. To the west are the great domes of Kata Tjuta (The Olgas), whose tallest unit, Mount Olga, is 200 metres higher than Uluru. These formations are the focus of spiritual belief for Anangu, the traditional indigenous guardians of the area.

Top, left: *An aerial view of Ormiston Gorge and Pound.*   **Top, right:** *Magnificent Kings Canyon, Watarrka National Park.*
Above: *Kata Tjuṯa (The Olgas), a group of gigantic sandstone domes, may be seen about 30 kilometres west of Uluṟu.*
Below: *The intensely coloured sandstone bluffs of Rainbow Valley, about 100 kilometres south of Alice Springs.*

Above: Perth city, seen over one of the many beds of wildflowers in Kings Park.

Below left: Looking down the line of beaches from Scarborough towards Cottesloe.   **Below right:** Hillarys Boat Harbour and Sorrento Quay, north of Perth.

Bottom, left: Fremantle, seen over Success and Fishing Boat Harbours.   **Bottom, right:** A view across Pinky Beach and Bathurst Light to Thomson Bay, Rottnest Island.

WESTERN AUSTRALIA

PERTH

Western Australia, the largest State, covers one-third of the continent and contains a vast variety of landscapes and scenic attractions. In the north are the splendours of the Kimberley. The north-west holds the spinifex-studded plains and rugged ranges of the Hamersley, the coral wonders of Ningaloo Marine Park, and the dolphins of Shark Bay. South of Perth, the capital, is the fertile south-west, with its vineyards, towering forests and spectacular coasts. Perth and its port, Fremantle, stand on the Swan River: their inhabitants enjoy the happiest of climates and have made their cities centres for arts, culture and cuisine. Nearby, bordering the Indian Ocean, are magnificent beaches, while Rottnest Island, just off the coast, is one of the nation's most favoured holiday destinations.

Top, left: *Perth at twilight, seen from Kings Park.* **Top, right:** *The Swan Bells, on the Swan River foreshore.*
Above, left and right: *The State's faunal and floral emblems: the Numbat and Red and Green Kangaroo Paw.*

Top: *The Busselton Jetty, once important in the life of a busy port.* **Above, left:** *Brookland Valley, a Margaret River winery.* **Above, right:** *Adventuring in the treetops in the Valley of the Giants, Walpole–Nornalup National Park.*

THE SOUTH-WEST

Favoured with plenty of rain and home to remarkable plant communities that range from brilliant wildflowers to some of the world's tallest trees, the south-west of Western Australia is a fascinating place. South of Perth, the towns of Bunbury and Busselton are popular seaside resorts. Margaret River is world-famous for its wines and surf beaches. The towering forests of the high rainfall areas are bordered by spectacular coastal scenery where wave-battered granite headlands shelter beaches of silver sand. A number of national parks runs across the State's southern coast, protecting areas of great natural beauty: the heathland inland from the beaches becomes a wildflower garden in spring and early summer. The Stirling Range National Park near Albany consists of a line of peaks famous for their diverse plant life. Further east, Fitzgerald River National Park is classified by UNESCO as a World Biosphere Reserve for its scenery, wildlife and flora.

Top: *The south coast's Stirling Range, seen here over pastureland, is famed for its spring displays of wildflowers.*
Above: *Sand dunes and an ocean beach in Fitzgerald River National Park.*
Below, left to right: *A variety of wildflowers including dampiera and everlasting daisies, Cowslip Orchids, Flame Pea.*

Top: *The Pinnacles, limestone formations in Nambung National Park, about 250 kilometres north of Perth.*
Above, left to right: *The Murchison River seen through Nature's Window, Kalbarri National Park; Bottlenose Dolphin; sea and sand, Francois Peron National Park, Shark Bay.*
Below: *Being a rider in a camel caravan on Cable Beach, Broome, is a great way to enjoy the sunset.*

The highway leading north from Perth is a road to adventure and discovery, at its most fascinating from August to October, when wildflowers carpet the coastal heath and woodland. The Pinnacles, pillars of limestone standing in Nambung National Park, are only the first wonders in a fascinating journey past fishing ports and rugged Kalbarri National Park to Shark Bay, where wild dolphins come to shore at Monkey Mia. The north-west of Western Australia is a region of ancient rocks, stark landscapes and rugged ranges. The mining towns are bases for exploration of wild places. Ningaloo Marine Park, on the seaward aspect of North West Cape, is a saltwater wonderland, while to the north, Broome, with its marvellous Cable Beach, is the gateway to the Kimberley. This northern region lies under the influence of the cyclonic monsoons that bring torrential rain during the high summer. The cooler Dry is the easier season in which to travel this land of boab trees and amazing landscapes.

Top: *Boab trees silhouetted against a dry-season sunset, the Kimberley.*
Above: *The remarkable striped domes of the Bungle Bungles, Purnululu National Park, mirrored in a billabong.*

AUSTRALIA'S NATIONAL FLAG has the British flag in the top left-hand corner with the seven-pointed Commonwealth Star beneath. It also bears the stars of the Southern Cross. This flag was formally established in 1953, being adopted from the Australian Blue Ensign, which was first flown in 1901.

AUSTRALIA'S COAT OF ARMS, designed in 1912, bears a Red Kangaroo and an Emu supporting a shield bearing the badges of the six States. The Crest of the arms is the seven-pointed, gold Commonwealth Star. The emblem also features branches of wattle tied with ribbon and a scroll bearing the word "Australia".

SOME STATISTICS

Population	18 972 350
Area of Australia	7 682 300 km²
Length of coastline	36 700 km

States and Territories	Area (km²)	Pop.
New South Wales	802 000	6 371 800
Victoria	227 600	4 644 950
Queensland	1 722 000	3 655 150
South Australia	984 000	1 467 300
Western Australia	2 525 500	1 851 300
Tasmania	68 300	456 700
Northern Territory	1 350 000	210 700
ACT	2 400	311 950

(2001 Census figures)

THE RED KANGAROO (*Macropus rufus*) that supports Australia's Coat of Arms is the largest kangaroo species, and it is found across much of the continent. It is generally regarded as being Australia's mammalian symbol,' and is noted for its hardiness, speed and unique appearance.

GOLDEN WATTLE (*Acacia pycnantha*) has been the official floral emblem of the Commonwealth of Australia since 1901. At least one species of wattle can be found in most regions of Australia; they are, as a group, particularly well-adapted to dry conditions and periodic droughts.

THE EMU (*Dromaius novaehollandiae*) is a large flightless bird that is found only in mainland Australia. It can survive adverse seasons and lives in most habitats except rainforest. The male Emu incubates the eggs and then looks after the striped chicks until they become independent.